The Nativity Pageant

Neil K. Johnson

CFI
An Imprint of Cedar Fort, Inc.
Springville, Utah

ISBN 13: 978-1-4621-2032-1

Published by CFI, an imprint of Cedar Fort, Inc.
2373 W. 700 S., Springville, UT 84663
Distributed by Cedar Fort, Inc., www.cedarfort.com

LIBRARY OF CONGRESS CATALOGING-IN-PUBLICATION DATA

Names: Johnson, Neil K., author.
Title: The Nativity pageant / adapted by Neil K. Johnson.
Description: Springville, UT : CFI, an imprint of Cedar Fort, Inc., [2017]
Identifiers: LCCN 2017027685 | ISBN 9781462120321 (saddlestitch)
Subjects: LCSH: Jesus Christ--Nativity--Drama. | LCGFT: Christmas plays.
Classification: LCC BT315.3 .J643 2017 | DDC 246/.72--dc23
LC record available at https://lccn.loc.gov/2017027685

Cover design by Shawnda T. Craig
Cover design © 2017 by Cedar Fort, Inc.
Edited and typeset by Kaitlin Barwick

Printed in the United States of America

10 9 8 7 6 5 4 3 2 1

Printed on acid-free paper

Contents

Praise for
The Nativity Pageant

Author and playwright, Neil Johnson, has accurately captured the simplicity and the glorious message from scriptural accounts of our Lord and Savior's birth. This pivotal moment in the great Plan of Salvation needs to be told, enacted, and presented again and again in family settings as well as in pageants for the education and edification of the public. This well-written and staged script makes this possible with simple props and alternate narrators that keep the focus on the greatest story ever told—that of the birth of our Savior, Jesus the Christ.

—Elaine S. Dalton, former General Young Women President

In a simple, clear, and professional way, Neil Johnson has dramatized the Christmas Story as it needs to be told. He draws directly from the scriptures in a way that will excite and inspire even young children. But for me, the greater blessing is it provides all the resources and tools necessary to create a very meaningful production of the Nativity. Everything is well organized to make our family time on Christmas Eve even more sacred and focused on our Savior and Redeemer, Jesus Christ.

—Larry M. Gibson, former member of the Young Men General Presidency

Neil Johnson's nativity play is concise, professional, and flexible. It helps to bring the meaning of Christ's birth into a format that is relatable and simple. The adjustable cast size makes it doable in a variety of settings. Neil's respect for the original story, combined with his vast drama experience, make this a valuable part of your church's or family's Christmas traditions.

—Melinda Lambert Baird, PhD, director of education and community outreach for Steinway & Sons

This lovely adaption of one of the most beautiful sections of the scriptures brings the poetic beauty of the message in Luke to show it in a simple, reverent way. It should be easy to perform and impactful in its simplicity and beauty.

—Brian Kelly, writer and editor of Church magazines and other LDS curriculum materials

General Instructions

Although the text is taken from the King James Version of the Bible, a few minor changes have been made for clarity and modern grammar.

Since this dramatization is for a simple but meaningful presentation in church or at home, it has the following:

1. Varying cast sizes, so this fits groups 6–25.
2. Simple stage directions, so this can be performed in any large room.
3. Two narrators to add interest for the audience.

Narrators and actors need to read loudly and clearly. However, they do not read the parts in parentheses. Those are stage directions for the actors.

Narrators 1 and 2 will have by far the most to read, so they should be good, loud readers. Narrators should sit at the side of the acting area.

There are 6 scenes with a total performance time of about 15 minutes, not counting the optional hymns. Select verses for the optional hymns appear in the appendix.

Character	Scene 1	2	3	4	5	6
Director*	x	x	x	x	x	x
Narrator 1*	x	x	x	x	x	x
Narrator 2*	x	x	x	x	x	x
Angel Gabriel*	x	x		x		x
Mary*	x		x	x		x
Joseph*		x	x	x		x
Donkey			x			
Shepherd(s)				x		
Other Angels				x		
King Herod*					x	
First Wise Man*					x	x
Other Wise Men					x	x
Chief Priest*					x	
Other Priests					x	
Stage Manager*	x		x		x	x
(Accompanist)*	x		x	x		x

(* will need script)

General Stage Areas

Up Right	Up Center	Up Left
Down Right	Down Center	Down Left

(Narrators)

Audience

Scene 1

Angel Gabriel and Mary

From Luke 1:26–38

(5 minutes plus optional hymn)

Props Needed:
Chair—center stage

Actors:
Angel Gabriel, Mary, Narrator 1, Narrator 2

Optional Hymn

Oh, Come, All Ye Faithful

(lyrics available in the appendix)

(*Stage manager places a chair in the center of the acting area.*)

Narrator 1 And in the sixth month the angel Gabriel was sent from God unto a city of Galilee, named Nazareth,

(*Mary enters and sits on the chair. She smiles, thinking of Joseph.*)

NARRATOR 2 To a virgin espoused to a man whose name was Joseph, of the house of David; and the virgin's name was Mary.

(*Angel Gabriel walks up to Mary.*)

NARRATOR 1 And the angel came in unto her, and said . . .

ANGEL Hail, thou that art highly favored, the Lord is with thee: blessed art thou among women.

(*Alarmed, Mary jumps up and hurries to the other side of the chair from Angel Gabriel.*)

NARRATOR 2 And when she saw him, she was troubled at his saying, and cast in her mind what manner of salutation this should be.

(*Mary keeps the chair between them. Angel Gabriel walks a few steps away from Mary, then turns toward her.*)

NARRATOR 1 And the angel said unto her . . .

ANGEL Fear not, Mary: for thou hast found favor with God. And, behold, thou shalt conceive in thy womb, and bring forth a son, and shalt call his name Jesus. He shall be great, and shall be called the Son of the Highest: and the Lord God shall give unto him the throne of his father David: And he shall reign over the house of Jacob forever; and of his kingdom there shall be no end.

(*Mary sits down again on the chair.*)

Narrator 2 Then said Mary unto the angel . . .

Mary How shall this be, seeing I know not a man?

(*Angel Gabriel smiles gently and walks over to Mary.*)

Angel The Holy Ghost shall come upon thee, and the power of the Highest shall overshadow thee: therefore also that holy thing which shall be born of thee shall be called the Son of God.

(*Mary puts her hands to her cheeks in amazement. Angel Gabriel walks a couple of steps away.*)

Angel And, behold, thy cousin Elisabeth, she hath also conceived a son in her old age: and this is the sixth month with her, who was called barren. For with God nothing shall be impossible.

(*Mary kneels at the feet of Angel Gabriel.*)

Mary Behold the handmaid of the Lord; be it unto me according to thy word.

(*Angel Gabriel smiles at Mary and exits.*)

Narrator 1 And the angel departed from her.

(*Mary exits. Stage manager removes the chair.*)

Scene 2

Angel Gabriel and Joseph

From Matthew 1:18–25
(2 minutes 30 seconds)

Props Needed:
Blanket

Actors:
Angel Gabriel, Joseph, Narrator 1, Narrator 2

(*Joseph enters with a blanket to center stage, lies down, and pretends to sleep.*)

Narrator 1	Now the birth of Jesus Christ was on this wise: When as his mother Mary was espoused to Joseph, before they came together, she was found with child of the Holy Ghost.
Narrator 2	Then Joseph her husband, being a just man, and not willing to make her a public example, was minded to put her away privately.

(*Angel Gabriel enters, walks over to Joseph, and looks down at him.*)

Narrator 1 But while he thought on these things, behold, the angel of the Lord appeared unto him in a dream, saying,

Angel Joseph, thou son of David, fear not to take unto thee Mary thy wife: for that which is conceived in her is of the Holy Ghost. And she shall bring forth a son, and thou shalt call his name Jesus: for he shall save his people from their sins.

(*Joseph wakes up and leans up on an elbow, looking up at the angel.*)

Narrator 2 Now all this was done, that it might be fulfilled which was spoken of the Lord by the prophet, saying . . .

Narrator 1 Behold, a virgin shall be with child, and shall bring forth a son, and they shall call his name Emmanuel, which being interpreted is, God with us.

(*Angel Gabriel exits. Joseph rubs his eyes and gets onto his knees as though praying.*)

Narrator 2 Then Joseph being raised from sleep did as the angel of the Lord had bidden him, and took unto him his wife.

(*Joseph stands, gathers his blanket, and exits.*)

Scene 3

Jesus Is Born in Bethlehem

From Luke 2:1–7

(3 minutes and 30 seconds plus optional hymn)

Props Needed:

Manger with a receiving blanket in it—down left, Doll—under Mary's robe

Actors:

Mary, Joseph, Donkey, Narrator 1, Narrator 2

(*Stage manager places the manger with the receiving blanket in it on down left corner.*)

Narrator 1 And it came to pass in those days, that there went out a decree from Cæsar Augustus, that all the world should be taxed.

Narrator 2 And all went to be taxed, every one into his own city.

(*Joseph leads the Donkey with Mary on its back to the down left corner of the acting area [or Joseph and Mary walk together]. Mary should tightly hold onto the actor playing the Donkey, and that actor should be careful that Mary doesn't lose her balance and fall off. Mary has the doll under her robe and over her tummy.*)

Narrator 1 And Joseph also went up from Galilee, out of the city of Nazareth, into Judæa, unto the city of David, which is called Bethlehem; because he was of the house and lineage of David:

(*Mary gets off the Donkey, stretches her painful back, and sits. The Donkey exits.*)

Narrator 2 To be taxed with Mary his espoused wife, being great with child.

Narrator 1 And so it was, that, while they were there, the days were accomplished that she should be delivered.

(*Mary pulls the doll out from her robe, lays him in the manger, tucks a receiving blanket around him, and stares at him lovingly.*)

Narrator 2 And she brought forth her firstborn son, and wrapped him in swaddling clothes, and laid him in a manger; because there was no room for them in the inn.

(*Joseph kneels next to Mary, also looking at the doll.*)

Optional Hymn

O Little Town of Bethlehem

Scene 4

Angels Tell Shepherds about the Baby Jesus

From Luke 2:8–19
(2 minutes and 30 seconds plus optional hymn)

Props Needed:
Manger—down left, Doll (remaining from Scene 3)

Actors:
Shepherds, Sheep, Angel Gabriel, Other Angel(s), Mary, Joseph, Narrator 1, Narrator 2

(*Shepherds enter and walk to stage right. Mary and Joseph stay kneeling at the manger down left.*)

Narrator 1 And there were in the same country shepherds abiding in the field, keeping watch over their flock by night.

(*Angel Gabriel enters up center.*)

Narrator 2 And, lo, the angel of the Lord came upon them, and the glory of the Lord shone round about them: and they were sore afraid.

(*Shepherds kneel or crouch in fear.*)

Narrator 1 And the angel said unto them . . .

Angel Fear not: for, behold, I bring you good tidings of great joy, which shall be to all people. For unto you is born this day in the city of David a Saviour, which is Christ the Lord. And this shall be a sign unto you; Ye shall find the babe wrapped in swaddling clothes, lying in a manger.

(*Other Angels enter and stand close to the first angel.*)

Narrator 2 And suddenly there was with the angel a multitude of the heavenly host praising God, and saying . . .

Other Angels (or Narrator 2)

Glory to God in the highest, and on earth peace, good will toward men.

Optional Hymn

Hark! The Herald Angels Sing

(*All Angels exit.*)

Scene 4

Narrator 1 And it came to pass, as the angels were gone away from them into heaven, the shepherds said one to another, "Let us now go even unto Bethlehem, and see this thing which is come to pass, which the Lord hath made known unto us."

(Shepherds go over to Mary and Joseph and kneel, looking at the baby Jesus.)

Narrator 2 And they came with haste, and found Mary, and Joseph, and the babe lying in a manger.

Narrator 1 And when they had seen it, they made known abroad the saying which was told them concerning this child.

(Shepherds rise and exit, pretending to be telling people about Jesus.)

Narrator 2 And all they that heard it wondered at those things which were told them by the shepherds.

(Mary looks at the baby Jesus, and then she stares up into the sky.)

Narrator 1 But Mary kept all these things, and pondered them in her heart.

(Mary picks up the doll, and she and Joseph exit. They leave the manger.)

SCENE 5

The Wise Men Meet King Herod

From Matthew 2:1–8
(2 minutes)

PROPS NEEDED:
Chair—up right

ACTORS:
King Herod, Wise Men, Chief Priest, Other Priest(s), Narrator 1, Narrator 2

(*Stage manager places chair on up right side.*)

(*King Herod enters and sits in chair. Wise Men enter from stage right and bow to him. They stay a little way away from him.*)

NARRATOR 1 Now when Jesus was born in Bethlehem of Judæa in the days of Herod the king, behold, there came wise men from the east to Jerusalem, saying . . .

1st Wise Man Where is he that is born King of the Jews? For we have seen his star in the east, and are come to worship him.

(*King Herod looks worried.*)

Narrator 2 When Herod the king had heard these things, he was troubled, and all Jerusalem with him.

(*Priests enter and walk to the left of Herod.*)

Narrator 1 And when he had gathered all the chief priests and scribes of the people together, he demanded of them where Christ should be born.

Narrator 2 And they said unto him . . .

Chief Priest In Bethlehem of Judæa: for thus it is written by the prophet: "And thou Bethlehem, in the land of Juda, art not the least among the princes of Juda: for out of thee shall come a Governor, that shall rule my people Israel." (*Micah 5:2*)

(*Priests exit.*)

(*King Herod motions for the Wise Men to come to him, and they do.*)

Narrator 1 Then Herod, when he had privately called the wise men, inquired of them diligently what time the star appeared.

Narrator 2 And he sent them to Bethlehem, and said . . .

King Herod Go and search diligently for the young child; (*Slyly says*) and when ye have found him, bring me word again, that I may come and worship him also.

(*King Herod and the Wise Men exit.*)

(*Stage manager removes chair.*)

Scene 6

The Wise Men Worship Jesus

From Matthew 2:9–15

(2 minutes plus optional hymn)

Props Needed:

Manger—down left (remaining from Scene 3), Gold, Frankincense, Myrrh, Doll

Actors:

Mary, Joseph, Wise Men, Narrator 1, Narrator 2

(Mary and Joseph enter and return down left to the manger, where they lay the doll down and stare at him.)

Narrator 1 When the wise men had heard the king, they departed; and, lo, the star, which they saw in the east, went before them, till it came and stood over where the young child was.

(*Wise Men enter upstage, following the star, and wander down right. One Wise Man points to the imaginary star down left.*)

NARRATOR 2 When they saw the star, they rejoiced with exceeding great joy.

(*The star leads the Wise Men to where Mary, Joseph, and the doll are. They kneel, looking at the doll.*)

NARRATOR 1 And when they were come into the house, they saw the young child with Mary his mother, and fell down, and worshipped him:

(*Wise Men kneel to worship, then they open their bag and present gifts.*)

NARRATOR 2 And when they had opened their treasures, they presented unto him gifts; gold, and frankincense, and myrrh.

(*Mary and Joseph happily accept the gifts.*)

(*Wise Men rise and exit.*)

(*Mary and Joseph lie down, asleep.*)

NARRATOR 1 And when the wise men were departed, behold, the angel of the Lord appeareth to Joseph in a dream, saying . . .

(*Angel Gabriel enters. Joseph awakens and listens.*)

Angel Arise, and take the young child and his mother, and flee into Egypt, and be thou there until I bring thee word: for Herod will seek the young child to destroy him.

(*Joseph stretches then wakes Mary. He gestures that an angel came. Mary fearfully picks up the doll, and they stand up.*)

Narrator 2 When he arose, he took the young child and his mother by night, and departed into Egypt:

(*Joseph and Mary exit.*)

Narrator 1 And was there until the death of Herod: that it might be fulfilled which was spoken of the Lord by the prophet, saying, "Out of Egypt have I called my son."

(*Angel Gabriel exits.*)

(*Optional: Entire cast enters to sing hymn.*)

Optional Hymn

Silent Night

Appendix
Hymn Lyrics

Oh, Come, All Ye Faithful

Hymn no. 202

Oh, come, all ye faithful,
Joyful and triumphant!
Oh, come ye, oh come ye to Bethlehem.
Come and behold him,
Born the King of angels;

[Chorus]

Oh, come, let us adore him;
Oh, come, let us adore him;
Oh, come, let us adore him,
Christ, the Lord.

O Little Town of Bethlehem

Hymn no. 208

O little town of Bethlehem,
How still we see thee lie.
Above thy deep and dreamless sleep
The silent stars go by;
Yet in thy dark streets shineth
The everlasting Light.
The hopes and fears of all the years
Are met in thee tonight.

Hark! The Herald Angels Sing

Hymn no. 209

Hark! the herald angels sing
Glory to the newborn King!
Peace on earth and mercy mild,
God and sinners reconciled!
Joyful, all ye nations, rise;
Join the triumph of the skies;
With th'angelic host proclaim
Christ is born in Bethlehem!

[Chorus]

Hark! the herald angels sing
Glory to the newborn King!

SILENT NIGHT

Hymn no. 204

1. Silent night! Holy night!
   All is calm, all is bright
   Round yon virgin mother and Child.
   Holy Infant, so tender and mild,
   Sleep in heavenly peace;
   Sleep in heavenly peace.

2. Silent night! Holy night!
   Shepherds quake at the sight!
   Glories stream from heaven afar;
   Heav'nly hosts sing Alleluia!
   Christ, the Savior, is born!
   Christ, the Savior, is born!

3. Silent night! Holy night!
   Son of God, love's pure light
   Radiant beams from thy holy face,
   With the dawn of redeeming grace,
   Jesus, Lord, at thy birth;
   Jesus, Lord, at thy birth.

About the Author

Neil K. Johnson

Neil Johnson and his current wife, Sharee, both lost their first spouses to cancer. They married and blended their family of fifteen kids, and they have fifty-two grandkids so far. Neil is very active in his church, and he always loves to see the enactment of the Nativity pageant at Christmastime. He knows many of the struggles to make the pageant meaningful, and he has tried to address them in this dramatization.

Neil taught school for forty-four years—first drama, then English—and he loves kids. He was chosen as the 2010 Utah English Teacher of the Year. Neil has written *The Drama Sourcebook* and has compiled three books containing thirty plays from other authors.

Neil and Sharee live in Lehi, Utah, within easy driving distance of most of their large family.

Scan to visit

www.neilkjohnsonauthor.com